THE *FANTASTIC* FOLD-OUT BOOK OF
Motor
RACING

JON KIRKWOOD

ALADDIN/WATTS
LONDON • SYDNEY

An Aladdin Book
© Aladdin Books Ltd 1997

Designed and
produced by
Aladdin Books Ltd
28 Percy Street
London W1P 0LD

ISBN 0 7496 2708 5

First published in Great Britain
in 1997 by
Aladdin/Watts
96 Leonard Street
London EC2A 4RH

Editor
Jon Richards

Design

David West
CHILDREN'S BOOK DESIGN
Designer
Flick Killerby

Illustrator
Peter Harper

Picture Research
Brooks Krikler Research

Printed in Belgium

Jon Kirkwood is a freelance author
and editor who has worked on a
number of books for children.

CONTENTS

THE FOLD-OUT SECTION

INTRODUCTION

For almost one hundred years, the world of motor racing has drawn people with its exciting mix of speed and danger. Since that time cars have been pushed to their limits in an attempt to beat the other competitors on the track. The sport has developed to such an extent that today's racing cars bear little resemblance to their predecessors. Speed is still the key, but the danger has been minimised by strict guidelines and high-tech safety measures.

Motor racing will take the reader around this high-octane world, where hundreds of different types of cars are pitted against each other in competitions of speed, agility and skill. These include dragsters, rally cars, go-carts and Le Mans racers. An eight-page fold-out section will show the stages of a Formula-One Grand Prix, from preparation and qualifying to the race itself and the winner's podium.

LE MANS RACING

Cars that take part in the GT (Grand Tourer) Endurance races need to be light-weight, reliable, incredibly powerful and able to stick to the road like glue. Perhaps the most famous of all GT Endurance races is the Le Mans 24-hour where teams of two or three drivers race cars over thousands of kilometres during the course of a night and a day.

Over the years, some of the greatest names in car-making have entered vehicles at Le Mans, including Porsche and Jaguar, whose *C-type* models *(above)* won many races in the early 1950s. Today's Le Mans racers, such as the McLaren *F1 GTR* and the Jaguar *XJR (right)* can reach speeds of 360 km/h (200 mph, *below*).

As opposed to the running starts that began the early Le Mans 24-hour race (see page 32), today's race begins with the cars lining up behind a pace car and making their way slowly around the track. When the pace car moves out of the way, the race begins (left). This is called a rolling start.

AERODYNAMICS

Racing car designers are forever searching for ways to make their cars sleeker, or more aerodynamic. As it drives along, a car that is not aerodynamic disturbs the smooth flow of wind over it, creating swirls and eddies. These disturbances of the airflow are called turbulence and they increase wind resistance, or drag on the car which slows it down. A racing car is designed to cut through the air without creating too much turbulence, letting the air flow smoothly over it. Such a car is described as aerodynamic.

Racing cars make use of the airflow to generate downforce. Wings attached to the racing car act like upside-down versions of an aircraft's wings, creating downforce instead of lift. This downforce presses the car tyres on to the track so they get better grip, allowing the racing car to go round corners faster and brake harder.

Some racing cars use air ducts at the front of the car ⬚1⬚ *(above) to generate even more downforce. In the McLaren F1 GTR (above) there are fans* ⬚2⬚ *which suck air from underneath. As a result, pressure beneath the car is reduced, increasing the effect of the downforce.*

A Formula-One car has wings on the front of its nose and a further wing on its rear to create downforce (below). These wings can be adjusted before a race to alter the amount of downforce needed. The downforce generated at 300 km/h (188 mph) is enough to stick the car to the ceiling!

Aerodynamic shape ensures car cuts through the air easily

Rear fins create downforce

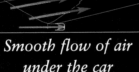

Smooth flow of air under the car

Rear wing

Front wings on a Formula-One car

Air-flow

Downforce

DRAG RACING

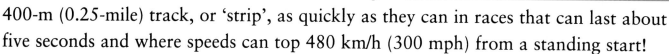

Drag racing is a flat-out challenge of speed and acceleration. Cars hurl themselves down a straight 400-m (0.25-mile) track, or 'strip', as quickly as they can in races that can last about five seconds and where speeds can top 480 km/h (300 mph) from a standing start!

A wide range of cars race at drag meetings, from the needle-like Top-Fuel dragsters (main picture) to Stock cars and the so-called 'Funny cars'. Despite this variety, all the models will have been stripped down to the bare essentials and fitted with amazingly powerful engines in an attempt to shave vital hundredths of a second off the time for each race.

FACT BOX

TOP-FUEL DRAGSTER

LENGTH: 7,620 MM (300 IN)
WIDTH: 1,420 MM (56 IN)
HEIGHT: 2,290 MM (90 IN)
WEIGHT: 955 KG (2,100 LB)
ENGINE TYPE: SUPERCHARGED, FUEL-INJECTED V-8
ENGINE SIZE: 8,200 CC (500 CU IN)
POWER: 6,500 BHP
BRAKES: HAND-LEVER ACTIVATED CARBON FIBRE DISCS, FRONT AND REAR, PLUS TWO PARACHUTES

BURNING RUBBER

At the start of a race, dragsters spin their wheels to improve tyre grip. This is called a burnout.

FUEL

Normal gasoline is not powerful enough to drive dragster engines. Instead, they use a variety of different fuels. The fastest cars, the Top-Fuel dragsters, burn a nitromethane mixture. Other cars use a mixture of alcohol and methane that does not deliver as much power but is a lot cheaper to use. In a single five second burst, a dragster engine can guzzle up to 57 litres (15 gallons) of fuel. With all this flammable liquid around, mishaps can occur *(below)*.

A turbocharger (below) is a device containing a turbine 1 turned by exhaust gases 2 from the engine. The turbine drives a blower 3 that compresses air and blows it into the engine increasing the pressure of the fuel/air mix 4, boosting power and improving fuel efficiency.

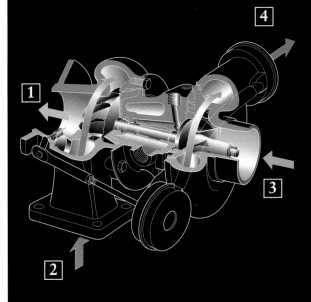

BOOSTING THE POWER

Turbochargers and superchargers are ways of greatly boosting an engine's power. For example, since turbos were banned from the sport in the late 1980s, a typical Formula-One engine can only produce 700 bhp – before they were banned a turbo-charged engine could produce 1,200 bhp!

Because turbochargers only work when the engine reaches a certain number of revs, the surge in power they deliver is delayed. Cars, such as dragsters, needing an immediate surge in engine power use superchargers. In these, the turbine is driven directly by the engine and not the exhaust gases. This boosts the power as soon as the engine is started.

GO-CART RACING

The small size of the vehicles used make cart racing a good place for the young driver to start in motor racing. Indeed, over half of today's Grand Prix drivers began competition behind the wheel of a cart. The small costs involved in carting make it one of the most popular forms of motor racing to take part in. Literally hundreds of different classes exist, determined by engine size, fuel type, driver's age, weight of the car and driver, etc...

It all adds up to an exhilarating sport where speeds can reach 256 km/h (160 mph)!

BRAKING AND SUSPENSION

Disc brakes **1** (*left*), where pads are squeezed against a disc that rotates with the wheel, are the most effective form of braking system. Because the disc can lose heat easily to the air it is less prone to 'fading' – where brakes become less effective because of the pad or shoe heating up. Drum brakes, where the brake 'shoes' are forced against the inside of a brake drum **2**, are less effective because they cannot lose heat as easily as disc brakes, making them more likely to 'fade'.

Car suspension has to deal with the bumps in the track, keeping the wheels in contact with it. Most car suspension has a spring **1** and a piston **2** inside an oil-filled cylinder **3** (*right*). Together, they compress and extend to absorb any bumps. Racing-car suspension (*above*) is stiffened, so that the car does not rock too much and can corner as quickly as possible.

Disc brakes

Brake pads

When the brakes of a car are applied they heat up due to friction between the brake pad and the wheel. In a racing car, they can glow red hot (right).

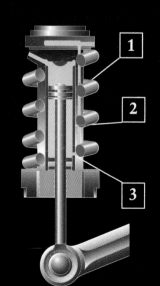

1
2
3

CARTING

Carts are raced with a minimum of bodywork – little attention is paid to the aerodynamic requirements of this vehicle. The most a cart might have are a bumper on the front and rear and two panels, one on either side. The engine sits behind or to one side of the driver. In the sport's early days, these engines were taken from old lawnmowers.

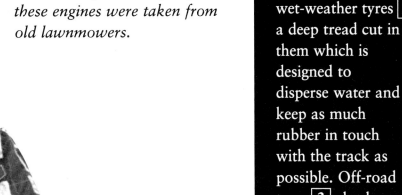

GETTING A GRIP

In dry weather (or indoors!) racing cars have slick tyres 1 (*below*), with no tread pattern, to get maximum grip. In the rain, however, cars change to special wet-weather tyres 2 . These have a deep tread cut in them which is designed to disperse water and keep as much rubber in touch with the track as possible. Off-road tyres 3 also have a deep tread to get the maximum grip while driving over rough terrain.

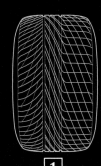

1

2

3

Cart racing is fast and furious, with cars usually bunched closely together as they hurtle around circuits that can be up to 1 km (0.6 miles) long (left). Because the performance of the carts in a class is pretty much the same, it is usually driver skill and daring that gets a cart to the front of the pack.

Go-cart circuit

R ALLY-CAR RACING

Driving beyond the comforts of a tarmacked race track, rallying is not a sport for the faint-hearted. Rally-cars fly along private roads, dirt tracks or across country, sometimes within a hair's breadth of trees or a sheer drop. Accidents are frequent *(left)*, but the cars are fitted with tough safety cages and harnesses to ensure the safety of those inside.

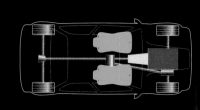

1 *In a four-wheel drive car all four wheels receive power from the engine which is often at the front of the car. However, some four-wheel drive cars have mid-mounted engines.*

Although they look similar to production cars, rally-cars differ greatly from road-going machines. They have to be specially prepared for the tough races. Engines are tuned and special racing gears *(see below)* are fitted. Many rally-cars also use four-wheel drive because this offers them the maximum grip when driving over conditions that can range from gravel to mud and even through water!

GEARS

A gearbox is a casing containing cogged wheels, called gears 1 *(above)*. These change the ratio of revolutions between input 2 and output 3 shafts, allowing the car to drive at different speeds. Some racing cars, such as Formula-One cars, are fitted with a semi-automatic gearbox. Instead of moving a cumbersome and time-consuming gear stick, the driver merely flicks a switch to change gear.

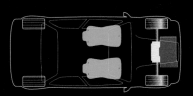

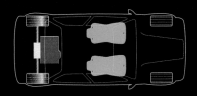

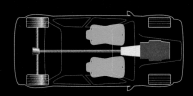

2 *A front-engined, front-wheel drive car is the most common orientation in many small road-going cars. Front-mounted engines tend to make cars more stable.*

3 *In a rear-engined car, an engine behind the driver drives the rear wheels. This configuration is common in high-performance cars, including Grand Prix cars.*

4 *Most road-going cars have an engine at the front driving the rear wheels. Putting the power on in a corner in a rear-wheel drive car tends to make the car oversteer.*

Rallying and off-road racing can take a hefty toll on a vehicle. After each stage the cars are stripped down (below) *and serviced, to ensure they deliver maximum performance for the next stage of the race.*

FACT BOX

RALLY-CAR
SUBARU IMPREZA 555

LENGTH: 4,340 MM
(171 IN)
WIDTH: 1,690 MM (67 IN)
HEIGHT: 1,390 MM (55 IN)
WEIGHT: 1,200 KG
(2,640 LB)
ENGINE TYPE: FUEL-
INJECTED, FOUR-CYLINDER
WITH TURBOCHARGER
ENGINE SIZE: 1,994 CC
(122 CU IN)
POWER: 300 BHP
BRAKES: VENTILATED DISCS
AND FOUR-POT CALLIPERS

FORMULA-ONE RACING

The shape of today's Formula-One racing car owes more to the aircraft industry than any other. The vehicle is packed with high-tech innovations from the carbon and aluminium honeycomb that makes up the sleek body to the sophisticated engine and the electronics that help control the car. However, many regulations have now been introduced restricting the use of electronics.

Cars are also fitted with a small black box recorder, similar to those used in all modern aircraft. This records all of the actions of the driver as well as data about the car. This information can then be used to spot what caused an accident.

Since the early days of motor racing, the shape of Formula-One cars has changed beyond recognition. Even in the 1950s, cars such as the Mercedes W196 (above) still had front-mounted engines. Today's rear-engined cars, such as the Ligier driven by Oliver Panis (below), are designed for a combination of speed, agility and safety.

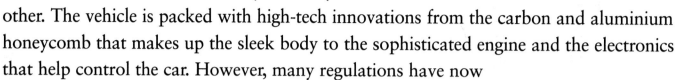

FACT BOX

**FORMULA ONE CAR
FERRARI 310**

LENGTH: 4,355 MM (171.5 IN)
WIDTH: 2,000 MM (78.7 IN)
HEIGHT: 950 MM (37.4 IN)
WEIGHT: 595 KG (1,310 LB) WITH WATER, OIL AND DRIVER
ENGINE TYPE: V-10
ENGINE SIZE: 2,998 CC (183 CU IN)
POWER: 700 BHP
BRAKES: CARBON DISCS AND PADS FRONT AND REAR

F1 COCKPIT

The driver of a Formula-One car is squeezed into a very tight cockpit *(right)*. In front of him there is an array of instruments that helps to control the car and keeps him informed about his performance. These instruments include warning lights that tell him when to change gear, an indicator of which gear the car is in and a selection of readouts that can include lap time and speed. There are controls to adjust the mixture of fuel and air in the engine's cylinders and to fine tune the strength of the car's brakes.

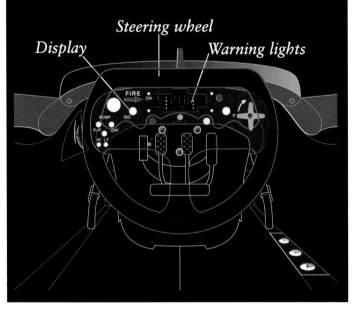

Display

Steering wheel

Warning lights

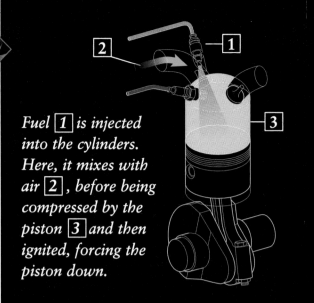

Fuel 1 *is injected into the cylinders. Here, it mixes with air* 2 *, before being compressed by the piston* 3 *and then ignited, forcing the piston down.*

FUEL INJECTION

Many racing cars have electronically controlled fuel-injected engines *(above)*. Fuel injection gives accurate control of the fuel-air mixture in the cylinder. A computer works out how much fuel is needed and when it should be injected into the engine's cylinders. It does this by measuring a number of factors when deciding how much and when to inject fuel. These include the level of engine revolutions per minute, the position of the throttle and the pressure of the air in the inlet system.

The computer is programmed before the race so that the demands for more power (a richer mixture) can be balanced against fuel economy (a leaner mixture) at all times.

Headphones in the driver's helmet relay instructions from the pit lane to the driver. At the same time, the car sends information through a radio link back to the pits where engineers can monitor its performance.

DRIVERS' PROTECTION

In the early days of racing competitors would drive wearing ordinary clothes. If there was an accident – especially a fire – there was no real protection for them. Today, however, drivers are covered from head to toe in clothing designed to keep them safe in the extreme heat and danger of a fire. Topping off the outfit is a light-weight, but extremely tough, crash helmet.

HEAD PROTECTION

Modern helmets weigh only 1.2 kg (2.6 lb) and have padded linings under the hard exterior. Some helmets are aerodynamically shaped to encourage airflow into the engine air inlet which is right behind the driver's head. Beneath the helmet, the driver's head is covered with a fire-resistant balaclava (*above*).

UNDER THE OVERALLS
A full set of fire-resistant underwear (left) is compulsory when you get into a Grand-Prix car. The long-sleeved top and full-length underpants are complemented by socks and the balaclava. Some drivers wear up to four layers of this protective clothing, leaving only the eyes uncovered.

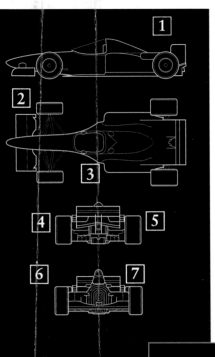

Race Day

When race day dawns, the excitement in the air is so intense that it charges every thought and action with extra meaning. Race day is the culmination of hours of preparation by the driver and the team. It is the time when the officials and marshalls at the track have to be ready to deal with the complexity and potential danger of a Formula-One race. Tension mounts throughout the day, peaking when lights signal the start of the race.

ADJUSTING THE CAR
The team have to keep an eye on the weather right up until the start of the race. Changes may include adjustment to the rear wing 1 *and the front wing size* 2 *to alter the amount of downforce. The engine cooling ducts on either side of the car are either covered (in rain) or are left open (in dry weather)* 3 *. Tyre pressure is higher in wet weather and lower in dry weather* 4 *. Varying thicknesses of brake discs* 5 *and the stiffness of the car's suspension* 6 *are selected depending on the demands of the circuit. The engine and gearbox* 7 *are set to produce the desired power output to suit the circuit.*

THE START
Once on the grid the cars will go on a single formation lap. Some drivers will use this to make sure their tyres are warm by weaving from side to side.

Once back at the grid, it's time to start the race. Drivers keep their revs high, waiting for the starting lights to go out (above), signalling the start of the race.

1   2   3

MORNING PRACTISE
In the morning before the race, drivers have a limited amount of time. During this period they can test their cars in full race set-up and see whether any further alterations are needed to make sure that they get the best performance for the conditions.

WINGS
Wings are adjusted to vary the amount of downforce. The multiple aerofoils of the rear wing give extra downforce over the whole speed range.

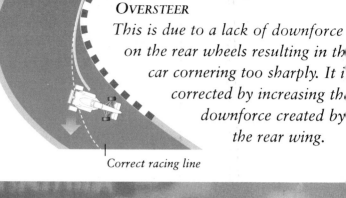

OVERSTEER
This is due to a lack of downforce on the rear wheels resulting in the car cornering too sharply. It is corrected by increasing the downforce created by the rear wing.

Correct racing line

Tyres warming up

TIMING
Throughout the course of the race the timing of a car is important, not just to confirm the driver's race position but in checking the car's performance. To measure their speed the cars are checked in three ways. A high-speed camera 1 *records the exact moment when a car passes. Sensors in the car* 2 *detect when it passes a certain spot. Sensors on the side of the track* 3 *record the time it takes a car to travel between two points.*

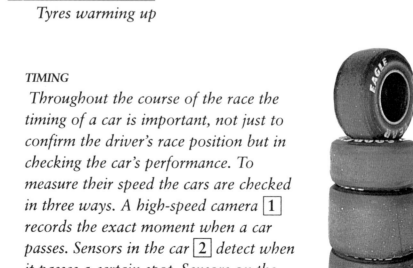

TYRES
Formula One tyres can either be slick or wet-weather (see page 11). They also come in different softnesses, or compounds, to suit different race conditions. In general, the softer the tyre, the better the grip. Before a race these tyres are heated in special blankets to around 100°C (212°F). Warming them helps to improve their grip.

Grand Prix

Teams will arrive at a circuit from the Wednesday before the race. In the period before race day on Sunday the pit area is busy as teams prepare the cars. Everything needed for the race has to be readily available. This includes: 1 Spare body parts and wings; 2 engines – up to ten engines may be used by each team; 3 spare wheels. Also required are computers, compressors and, of course, tools.

Today's Formula-One teams carry about 25 tonnes of cars and equipment to each race in massive, specially built container lorries (below).

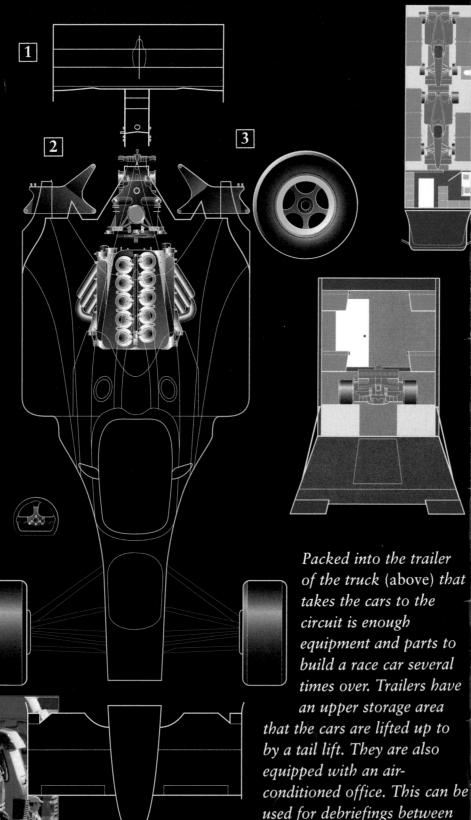

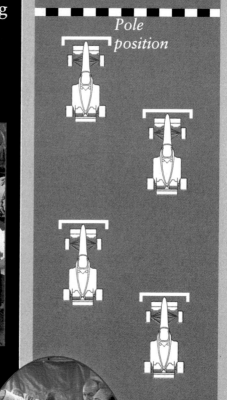

Packed into the trailer of the truck (above) that takes the cars to the circuit is enough equipment and parts to build a race car several times over. Trailers have an upper storage area that the cars are lifted up to by a tail lift. They are also equipped with an air-conditioned office. This can be used for debriefings between engineers and drivers during the time at the circuit.

Qualifying

On the days before the race, drivers have two practice sessions where they can test the performance of their cars. The Saturday afternoon before the race is the qualifying period. For one hour only, drivers have 12 laps to record their fastest lap. This time will decide their position on the grid – the quickest driver will start in pole position *(below right)*.

Throughout this qualifying period the cars are fitted with special engines tuned for qualifying and they run with fuel tanks that are very nearly empty to keep the weight down and the speed up.

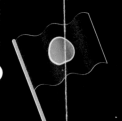
Pole position

Before, during and after qualifying, the teams will scrutinise masses of information about both the car and the driver's performance (above and right). This information will include technical data about the car, such as fuel consumption, power output, lap times and video of how the driver performed around the track. All of this is used to improve performance and grab that vital pole position.

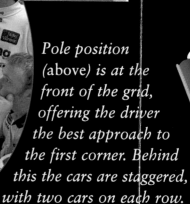

Pole position (above) is at the front of the grid, offering the driver the best approach to the first corner. Behind this the cars are staggered, with two cars on each row.

End of race

Danger

Mechanical problem

All clear

The race has been stopped

UNDERSTEER

This is due to a lack of downforce on the front wheels resulting in the car drifting wide on a corner. It is corrected by increasing the downforce created by the front wings.

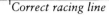

Correct racing line

Changing tyres

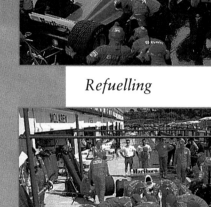

Refuelling

Changing nose cone

Pit stops

Perhaps one of the most exciting moments in a Formula One race is the pit stop. With the car off the track, vital time is being lost and it is important to get the car racing again as soon as possible.

Once the car has stopped a team of nearly 20 mechanics swarm around it *(left)*. They will be busy changing tyres, refuelling the car or occasionally replacing damaged pieces of the car's body, such as the nose cone. Depending on the amount of work that needs doing to a car, a well-drilled pit team can have the car ready in as little as seven seconds!

BOARDS AND RADIO LINKS

The driver is in constant communication with the team in the pits. They talk to him via a radio link. To back up radio communication, a board is used that tells the driver his position, how fast his last lap was and whether to come into the pits.

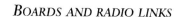

RETIREMENT

On average only half the cars that start a race cross the finishing line. The most common cause of retirement is collision. Other causes include punctures, spinning off, engine failure, transmission breakdown and electrical problems.

WINNING THE RACE

In general, the first driver past the chequered flag wins the race (left). There are, however, several tests that the car must undergo before the winner is confirmed (see page 23). Once this has been done the award ceremony can take place, with the first three drivers standing on the podium while the winner's national anthem is played. These three drivers will then take great delight in spraying each other, and anyone else who's in range, with champagne (right).

OVERTAKING AND SLIPSTREAMING

During a race, a driver not only has to get around a track, he must avoid and overtake other drivers as well. Methods of overtaking include 'slipstreaming'. This involves the following car tucking in behind the one in front. Here the following car is sheltered from turbulence. At the right moment he can pull out and, with a burst of power, overtake.

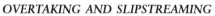

e Race Officials

...re a number of flags used
...ials to let drivers know
...ace conditions (left), such
...ppery surface, or to give
...n instructions and
...formation, including warning
...hem of unsportsmanlike
behaviour. The one every
driver wants to see is the
chequered flag.

One of the duties of the officials is checking the driver's
performance (*below*) and the car after the race (*above*) to
make sure that they have conformed to the rules. Among
other things they will check that the correct type of fuel
has been used and also examine a device attached to the
underside of each car. This device is used to stop the cars
riding below the minimum legal height for the base of the car,
which is 10 mm (0.3 in).

| 1 | 2 | 3 |

*In a collision, the blame depends upon the
situation. In 1 (above) it is the fault
of the blue car because he has not
got far enough up on the car in
front and cannot claim the racing
line. In 2 the responsibility is
shared because both cars have
equal claim to the racing line. In 3
the red car is at fault because the blue
car has gained enough ground to claim
the racing line.*

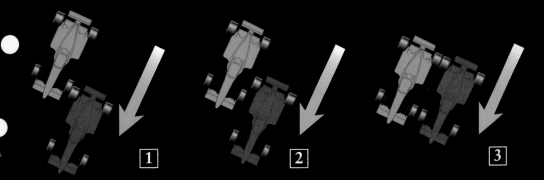

...vehicle
...ck

The Aftermath

*The goal of every Formula-One driver is
to win the Drivers' Championship.
Points are awarded for
different finishing positions
and over the season these
are added together. The
driver with the most
points at the end of the
season wins the Drivers'
Championship (right).*

As soon as the race is over and the car has been checked
by officials, the team begins the hurried process of
packing their equipment back into the trucks (*above*).
Speed is of the essence as the sooner they can get
back to their base factory, the more time they have
to work on the car, revising and altering its
performance, before the next race.

THE RACE TEAMS
The Constructors' Championship is
where the points that the team's two
drivers gather are added together. The
most successful teams are Ferrari and
McLaren who have both won nine
championships. The teams are
recognisable from the colours of their
cars and the drivers' overalls.

Williams   Ligier   Jordan   McLaren   Williams   Benneton

*Within two hours of the end of a race
all of the equipment has been
hurriedly packed away into the
lorries. Over a season, each race
team, along with its cars, tools
and parts, will travel over
160,000 km (100,000
miles) moving between
the circuits and the team's
base factory.*

THE RACE TEAM

On raceday, the driver and mechanics are just the most visible people in the team. There are a great many people involved behind the scenes. These range from those people who look after the team's catering to those who do the computer designing for the car's bodywork. A large number of people are also involved with the companies that construct the race engines.

THE RACE TEAM
Up to fifty people are involved in each Formula One Team. These include: two mechanics responsible for tyres; two mechanics responsible for fuel; ten technicians watching telemetry monitors; one spares manager; four mechanics for each car; two people responsible for cleaning and logistics; and two race drivers.

THE DRIVERS
Below is a list of some of Formula One's greatest drivers of the past and possibly of the future. Some have been successful in more than one form of motor sport. For example, Nigel Mansell and Jacques Villeneuve have been successful in both Formula One and Indy car racing.

SPONSORSHIP
Formula-One motor racing is a very expensive undertaking. Sponsorship is a vital way of raising money to fund the teams. As such, the cars, the mechanics and the drivers' overalls are covered in company logos (left).

Juan Fangio

Stirling Moss

Jack Brabham

Nikki Lauda

Ayrton Senna

Nigel Mansell

Jacques Villeneuve

BEYOND FORMULA ONE

Outside the world of Formula One, safety plays just as important a role. Dragsters, saloon cars, rally cars and stock cars are fitted with a safety cage which surrounds the driver. Dragsters are also fitted with an in-car fire extinguisher system which sprays both the engine and the cockpit. They also have an escape hatch in the roof.

At positions around the circuit, marshals are stationed where they can wave flags to warn drivers and assist in an emergency. There are also specially equipped fire marshals (right) *who can respond to a fire within seconds.*
Cranes may also be available to lift a damaged car clear of the track (above).

SAFETY IN RACING

Of paramount importance to all concerned in motor racing, in all its forms, is safety. This is not just the safety of the drivers but also of the spectators, race officials and team members.

Technological advances have led to the fitting of black box recorders to racing cars *(see page 14)*. Super-strong materials are now used to make a racing car's body, forming a protective shield around the driver. Other, more simple ideas have also been introduced. These include the use of gravel traps which can slow cars quickly and tyre walls which can absorb much of the force of an impact.

HARNESSED

Drivers have a full six-point safety harness to keep them securely restrained in the cockpit. Like other safety features and equipment, the harness must be approved by the FIA, the official body of motor racing. There is a quick release in the centre of the harness so the driver can get out of the car quickly when it stops. Some racing cars are also fitted with a removable steering wheel (*right*) which can be easily pulled out in the event of a crash to let the driver escape quickly.

Pace cars (below) are brought on to the track in most forms of racing if an accident occurs. The remaining cars must form up behind this slow-moving vehicle until the problem has been cleared. The pace car then moves out of the way and the race begins again.

To warn drivers about the presence of a slow or official vehicle on the track, the marshals wave white flags. If the accident is very severe the race may be stopped all together.

ROLL BARS

In many forms of motor racing, drivers are protected by a roll bar (*left*). This can be as simple as a single hoop of steel which sits just behind the driver's head. Should the car flip over, this simple yet strong device stops the driver from being squashed.

The roll bar in a Formula-One car is built into the bodywork in an unobtrusive manner, sitting around the engine air intake. Along with the tough carbon-fibre casing which surrounds the driver, this makes the cockpit of a Formula-One car virtually indestructible.

THE WORLD'S CIRCUITS

Most race circuits in the world – apart from the oval tracks used in Indy racing – are a combination of straights, where the cars accelerate up to their top speed, and different types of bends. The circuits are designed to give cars and drivers an all-round test so that top speed is not the most important factor. Handling around the bends can become just as important. Different types of bends call for different techniques from the drivers.

Most circuits are in country areas where there is plenty of space but there are also some circuits that are in towns or cities, such as the Monaco Grand Prix *(see page 31).*

S-BEND

S-BEND
At an S-bend a driver brakes before turning into the first of the two bends. He then accelerates through and out of the second bend (above).

MONTRÉAL
Canada
4.43 km (2.77 miles)

START/FINISH LINE   CHICANE

PIT LANE

CHICANE
The chicane is a series of tight turns in opposite directions in an otherwise straight stretch of a track. To stay as fast as possible drivers have to keep braking to a minimum amount and try to 'straighten out' the bend by picking the best racing line (right).

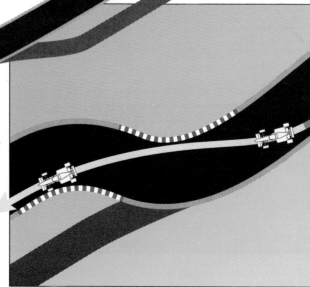

SILVERSTONE
GREAT BRITAIN
5.226 km (3.266 miles)

HOCKENHEIM
GERMANY
6.802 km (4.25 miles)

SPA-FRANCORCHAMPS
BELGIUM
6.94 km (4.34 miles)

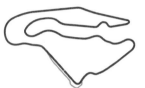

MAGNY-COURS
FRANCE
4.271 km (2.669 miles)

MONZA
ITALY
5.8 km (3.625 miles)

ESTORIL
PORTUGAL
4.35 km (2.72 miles)

SUZUKA
JAPAN
5.864 km (3.665 miles)

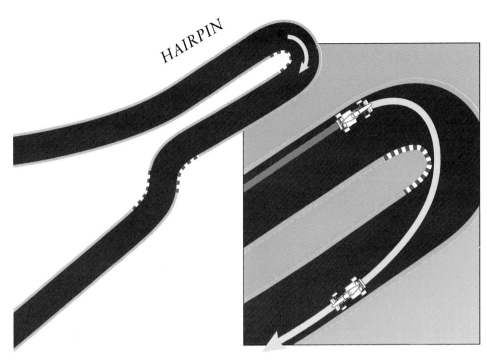

HAIRPIN

HAIRPIN

A hairpin is a U-shaped turn in a track where the cars turn by 180 degrees (above). Drivers have to brake hard and then turn late. As they move around the bend they accelerate before straightening.

THE PITS

In the pits of any race the mechanics play a vital role in keeping the car on the track. In a Formula One race the pit crew can be huge (about 20), but in Indy racing the permitted pit crew is just two mechanics (*below*). All the mechanics wear protective overalls, made from Nomex, the same material used to protect the drivers (see page 16).

To ensure safety in the pits, Formula One drivers must keep below 120 km/h (75 mph). Anyone breaking this rule faces stern time penalties.

SALOON CARS
Modified road-going cars are used in saloon-car racing (*left*). However, major alterations have to be made to them. These will include fitting safety cages, a race-tuned engine, racing seats and driver harnesses. Car-to-car contact is common and cars will often nudge each other, especially when cornering, to gain an advantage.

ROUND THE BEND

There is a wide diversity of lap-style motor races from the all-out oval-circuit racing of the Indy races to the tortuous town races in cities such as Monaco. Some of the fiercest racing takes place using cars that are recognisable as cars you might be able to buy and run on the street. And some only slightly modified vehicles engage in a crash-filled spectacle of stock-car racing that can result in very few finishers, such as the American NASCAR series (*right*).

OVAL CIRCUITS
In banked oval circuits, cars do not have to slow down as much for corners as they do on non-banked circuits. This is because the banking counteracts some of the forces created by the car turning. To give them further help around the banked corners, Indy drivers can raise one side of their car using compressed air.

CITY-BASED RACES

Racing around a city, as with the Grand Prix de Monaco *(right)*, has its thrills and special problems for the driver. It is very hard, for instance, to overtake when races are held in narrow streets. At such a race, getting pole position is very important. There are other hazards with city-based races. Should the driver come off the track, there is no run-off area and the car will hit a wall or a barrier instead of coming to rest on gravel or grass.

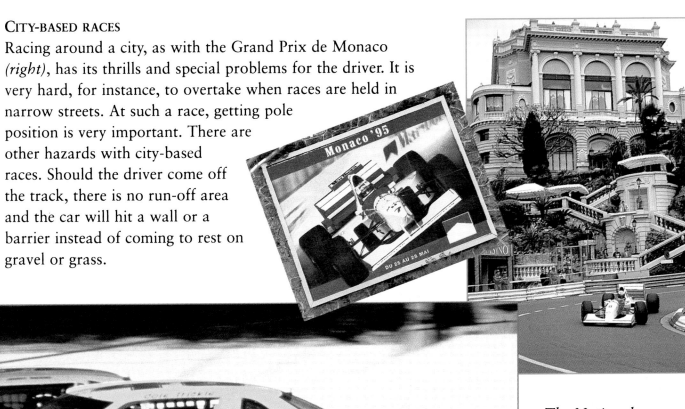

The National Association for Stock Car Racing (NASCAR) holds races for saloon cars around oval tracks. These cars regularly record lap speeds in excess of 322 km/h (200 mph).

INDY RACING

In Indy racing, cars hurtle at high speed around oval circuits *(right)*. The test is of speed, stability and nerve. The cars are not that different to Formula One. The sport is named after the Indianapolis Motor Speedway at Speedway, near Indianapolis, Indiana. The 4-km (2.5-miles) track, nicknamed the 'Brickyard', is the oldest motor racing track still in use. It is the venue for the Indianapolis 500.

GOING THE DISTANCE

With endurance races, the emphasis isn't so much on speed, as it is on actually completing the race, keeping both driver and machine going until the finish. These races include the non-stop 24-hour races such as Le Mans, and the rallies that can cover huge distances in separate stages over roads, tracks or across country.

At the end of every Monte Carlo Rally competitors have to race in a hill-climb section where they are timed up a course through the surrounding hills (below).

Early Le Mans races would start with the drivers sprinting across the track to their cars (left). However, this has since been replaced by a rolling start (see page 6).

RALLY NAVIGATION

Seemingly alone in the middle of nowhere, a car on a long-distance rally raises a cloud of dust as it navigates between checkpoints *(left)*.

Getting lost is one of the major hazards of long-distance rallying and the role of the navigator is made doubly important as time is precious. A wrong turning can cost vital seconds, minutes, hours or even days!

Perhaps the most famous of all rallies is the Monte Carlo Rally (below). Since it began in 1911, hundreds of competitors have started from different points throughout Europe and North Africa heading for Monte Carlo. Weather conditions have always proved a key factor in this winter rally. So much so, that in the 1965 race, only 22 cars out of 237 finished the race.

RALLYING

Rallying has a long history and began way back in 1907 with a race between Peking and Paris. It took competitors over 60 days to cover a distance of 12,000 km (7,500 miles). The East African Safari, which was first run in 1953, is the longest rally that is held regularly – it covers a mighty 6,234 km (3,874 miles).

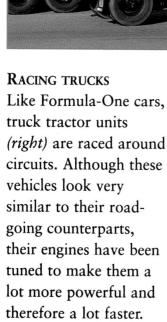

Racing Oddballs

If it has wheels and a motor, the chances are that someone has raced it. Everything from production cars straight off the street to special models made for hill climbing, giant trucks, tractor units of freight lorries and veteran three-wheelers has been or is a part of the race scene – some people will even race lawn mowers!

People will go to amazing lengths to alter their vehicles. In this case (above) *a truck has been fitted with counterweights to let it pull 'wheelies'. Some trucks have even been fitted with jet engines. One, called* Shockwave, *can reach 605 km/h (376 mph).*

RACING TRUCKS
Like Formula-One cars, truck tractor units *(right)* are raced around circuits. Although these vehicles look very similar to their road-going counterparts, their engines have been tuned to make them a lot more powerful and therefore a lot faster.

MONSTER TRUCKS AND RACING TRACTORS

Some of the most extraordinary machines used in 'races' are found in dirt-filled arenas. So-called Drag Tractors bear little resemblance to the farming vehicles (*left*). In a trial of strength, these powerful tractors try to pull increasingly heavier loads over a set distance. Monster trucks (*below*) are basically normal trucks fitted with huge wheels, enormous suspension and a powerful engine. These vehicles are raced around dirt tracks, leaping over obstacles and crushing cars.

A SMASHING TIME

Some 'races' are little more than trials by combat where cars deliberately smash into each other on a mud or dirt track until there is only one left that can actually continue moving. This car is declared the 'winner'. The cars used for these races are prepared to make them safe for the driver, with harnesses and safety cages. However, not much effort is spent making the bodywork look attractive (*right*).

35

RACING HISTORY

Almost as soon as motor cars became practicable, they were being raced. Racing satisfies not only the competitive instincts but it is a means whereby car manufacturers can test out new technology. Over the years, this desire for competition has led to the development of many different forms of racing all over the world.

By pushing engines and other components to their limits, car makers have learned how to make cars not only faster but also more economical, more efficient and more reliable. So racing has been of great importance in furthering the development of automobiles generally.

The first Grand Prix race was held in France in 1906 at Le Mans, France (above). *The winning driver was Ferenc Szisz* (below) *driving a Renault. He led a field that included 34 cars, 25 of them French and nine being German and Italian. The race was held on two succesive days and involved six laps of an enormous 103-km (64-mile) circuit.*

LE MANS: THE BENTLEY YEARS

One of the dominating forces at Le Mans during the 1920s was the British Bentley team. Since the first 24-hour race in 1923 until the close of the decade, Bentleys won five of the races, losing in 1925 and 1926 to the Lorraine Dietrich team. The picture (*above*) shows a Bentley in the 1930 race, a race that was to be their last success at the historic meeting.

The changing appearance of racing cars can be seen in this 'parade' (below), ranging from the Sunbeam Tourist to the Mclaren Ford.

RACING IN AMERICA

One of the first car races on the American continent were the Vanderbilt Cup races. Launched in 1904, the races were held over a triangular course on Long Island, the first being won by American George Heath driving a Panhard.

Since that time, the number and type of races has multiplied. Perhaps the most famous on the continent being the Indianapolis 500 (so called because the race was over 500 miles). The first of these races was held on 30 May 1911, when American Ray Harroun won driving a Marmon Wasp.

The picture (*above*) shows an alarming incident from the 1932 race, when Billy Arnold crashed. Other races included the Santa Monica Grand Prix, which had the famous 'Death Curve'. Here (left) Johnny Marquis crashes during the 1914 race.

1914 Sunbeam Tourist

1950 Alpha Romeo 158

1954 Mercedes W196

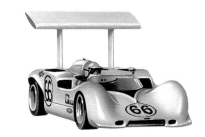

Chaparral 2E

DURING THE WARS

Most forms of motor racing were postponed during the two World Wars. Instead of producing more racing cars, many factories and workshops were turned over to producing munitions (*left*). Grand Prix racing began in 1921 after World War I and in 1947 after World War II.

1969 Matra

1973 McLaren-Ford

GLOSSARY

Aerodynamics
The science of how objects move through the air. In motor racing, an aerodynamic car is one that slips through the air, creating little turbulence, or drag.

Aerofoil
In motor racing, a wing that provides downforce as the car moves through the air.

Axle
This can be a shaft on which a wheel revolves, a revolving shaft with a wheel on it or a rod connecting two wheels.

Bore
The diameter of a cylinder in an engine.

Burnout
In drag racing, the spinning of tyres while the vehicle is stationary before a race to get them to the temperature where they give the most grip.

Calliper
A braking component in which friction plates press against a rotating disc.

Capacity
The size of the engine. It is the amount of air that is displaced by the engine's cylinders during a single cycle.

Chassis
The supporting framework for the car's body, engine and suspension of a car. In many racing cars it is a frame made from metal tubes.

Cockpit
The space for the driver, controls and instruments.

Connecting rod
The connecting or 'con' rod links the piston to the crankshaft in an engine.

Cylinder
A hollow chamber found in engines in which a piston slides back and forth.

Downforce
A force created by the wings or bodywork of a car as it moves through the air. It pushes down on the car, improving its roadholding ability.

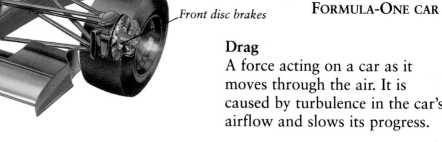

Rear wing

V-10 engine

Rear disc brakes

Safety harness

Front disc brakes

Nose cone

Front wing

FORMULA-ONE CAR

Drag
A force acting on a car as it moves through the air. It is caused by turbulence in the car's airflow and slows its progress.

Engine
The device that turns energy into force or motion. An internal combustion engine, such as a petrol or diesel engine, converts energy released by burning of the fuel inside its cylinders into motion.

Fade
The tendency of brakes to become less efficient after repeated use because of heating of the braking surfaces.

Fuel injection
This gives accurate control of the fuel-air mixture in the cylinder. In many cars, a computer calculates how much fuel is needed and when it should be injected for optimum performance.

Gearbox
The casing containing gears which change the ratio of revolutions between input and output shafts.

Pole position
The number one position at the front of a racing grid.

Roll cage
The framework built into a car to protect the driver in the event of a crash.

Shock absorber
A device that absorbs sudden shocks to the suspension of the vehicle.

Slick
A tyre with no tread, and usually made of a soft compound for maximum grip.

Suspension
A system of devices – usually springs, linkages and shock absorbers – that supports the upper part of a vehicle on its axles.

Transmission
A system of shafts and gearboxes that transmits power from the engine to the axle of the vehicle.

Turbine
A device comprising a shaft fitted with blades that is turned by the flow of a liquid such as water or a gas such as steam through it.

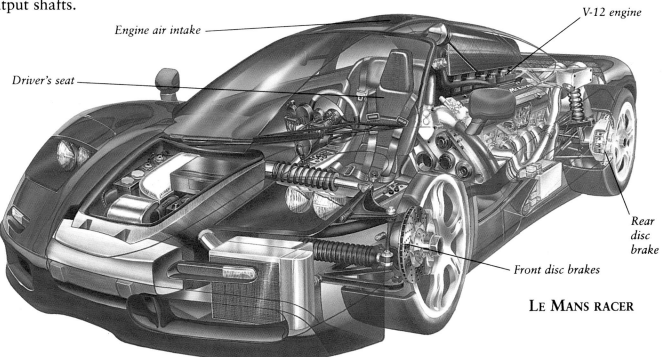

Engine air intake

V-12 engine

Driver's seat

Rear disc brake

Front disc brakes

LE MANS RACER

Methanol
A type of alcohol that is used as a fuel in certain racing cars.

Nitromethane
Also known as 'nitro', a fuel component that gives enhanced performance.

Piston
A disc or cylinder that fits tightly within a cylinder and moves back and forth.

Stroke
The distance the piston travels up and down in a cylinder.

Supercharger
A device which blows air into the engine inlet to boost its power. It contains a fan driven by mechanical linkage from an engine.

Turbocharger
A device containing a fan that is driven by a turbine by exhaust gases from the engine. The turbocharger blows air into the engine, raising the pressure of the fuel-air mixture in the cylinders, boosting the engine's power output.

Wheelbase
The distance between the front and rear axles of a vehicle.

Index

Photo Credits:

Abbreviations: t-top, m-middle, b-bottom, r-right, l-left
Front cover – Honda UK. 3, 4-5, 10 both, 11 both, 14m, 14-15, 15t, 16 all, 17, 18m & b,
23b, 24m, 25t, m & b far r, 26mr & b, 27 all, 29 both, 30b, 31tl & b & 33t – Empics.
6t & b, 7b, 8-9, 19, 20m & b, 24t & bl & 26t – Rex Features. 6m, 14t, 20t, 20-21, 21t,
mt, mb & bl & 23t – Zooom Photographic. 6-7, 12tl, 12-13, 13b, 18t, 21br, 22 all,
25bcr, 26ml, 28, 31tr, 32b, 35 all & back cover – Frank Spooner Pictures. 7t – Mercedes
Benz Foto. 8t & 9 all – Neil Smith. 13m & 30t – Ford UK. 24br, 25br, 34 both & 34-35
– Eye Ubiquitous. 25b far r, bl & bc, 32m, 32-33t, 36 all, 36-37 & 37b – Hulton Getty
Collection. 25bcl & 32-33b – Solution Pictures. 30-31 – British Film Institute.
37t – Mary Evans Picture Library.